Table Of Contents

Copyright © 2010-Present. Hyperink Inc.

The standard legal stuff:

All rights reserved. No part of this book may be reproduced in any form or by any electronic or mechanical means, including information storage and retrieval systems, without permission in writing from Hyperink Inc., except for brief excerpts in reviews or analysis.

Our note:

Please don't make copies of this book. We work hard to provide the highest quality content possible - and we share a lot of it for free on our sites - but these books are how we support our authors and the whole enterprise. You're welcome to borrow (reasonable) pieces of it as needed, as long as you give us credit.

Thanks!

The Hyperink Team

Disclaimer

This ebook provides information that you read and use at your own risk.

We do not take responsibility for any misfortune that may happen, either directly or indirectly, from reading and applying the information contained and/or referenced in this ebook.

Thanks for understanding. Good luck!

CHECK OUT MORE TITLES FROM OUR BEST BOOK SERIES!

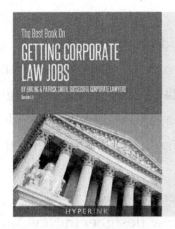

The Best Book On Getting Corporate Law Jobs

Want to learn the exact steps to getting a prestigious corporate law job? Interested in working for Davis Polk, Wilson Sonsini, and other top firms? Hear directly from the students that got in!

$25

BUY NOW

The Best Book On Getting An IBanking Internship

Applying to Goldman Sachs, Morgan Stanley, and JPMorgan? A bulge-bracket intern shares her advice on how you can break into investment banking! This ebook covers everything from resumes to interviews to firm cultures.

$25

BUY NOW

The Best Book On Naturopathy

Interested in becoming a naturopath? Julie Tran shares her stories and strategies for becoming a naturopathic doctor!

$25

BUY NOW

About The Author

Can't remember what you had for lunch yesterday?
I can.

I can remember what you had for lunch yesterday, and what you had for dinner at that shack on a deserted beach in Bali seven years ago. And what I had that day I came back from sightseeing to a B&B in Telc, Czechloslovakia, and found homemade garlic toasted cheese sandwiches waiting in the kitchen with thick hot chocolate on the side.

I always remember what everyone had. I just do.

On the outside, I was a lighting designer in New York theater and for private clients. But on the inside, I was on my own private eat quest.

I would go to a farmer's market and come back with pecorino fresca and a hot tip on where to find lobster mushrooms in a remote corner of upstate New York.

My passion for all things food led to reading and writing about it on various online food chat rooms. Before long, I found myself the go-to source for a growing circle of friends on the hunt for a cool night out, soon followed by celebrities from my day job seeking a totally unique experience, off the beaten path of the already (in)famous overpriced restaurants. I love telling people where to dine, or setting up a fun evening from an aperitif to an after dinner cigar.

My own private eat quest has blossomed into eatquestnyc, a full-fledged global dining service, matching the right meal with the right diner, fulfilling any craving from ingredient searches to planning parties, food crawls – and even an at home proposal dinner. I love to personally curate your food experience, big or small, quirky or simple. For me it's a dating service for people and their food. A twist on a matchmaking site. I cover the waterfront featuring an array from premium, to intimate, to cool casual, even when you know a mean burger in Brooklyn but want to outdo yourself in the Bronx.

Here is what I have learned so far on my eat quest. It may help you on yours. And don't forget to tell me what you had for lunch yesterday.

Food Writing 101

What Is Food Writing?

Food writing is about words you can almost taste. Food is about more than sustenance, it's an emotional connection, it relates to culture, memory, kinship and as writers we invite our readers along to join us for pleasurable, surprising and unique adventures. A food writer is charged with steering the public toward a satisfying cultural experience – the perfect meal. Food criticism is perhaps the most engaged and visceral type of criticism; it relies on that most sensual and crucial of public activities … eating.

A writer needs to articulate *why* this dish. Why is your shrimp risotto better? Is it the creaminess of the rice infused with chopped shrimp? A Proustian moment about your first risotto? A secret herb slipped into the mix? It's not just writing about the good itself, it's the stories your share about your experience as a diner, food lover, human being that creates the whole.

It's how you consider food, what it means to you, and what ultimately becomes your voice that sets you apart from others. The most important thing is – ENJOY what you do. Then others might as well. As Julia Child said: "What keeps me motivated is not the food itself, but all the bonds and memories the food represents."

When I wrote about a favorite Chinese restaurant, I was innundated by clients and friends who had to have Chinese food now. The big trick is to make people want what you have had. You want to trigger the impulse to go from thinking about what you said to doing what you say. Make your reader feel like they are at the table with you and are just about to be offered a bite!

Words like delicious don't work anymore; be specific, not clichéd, and don't over-describe. Food is passionate and intimate and soul-satisfying, so use words that are illustrative and have an emotional resonance for your reader.

Food Critics Vs. Food Writers

The term "food writer" is often used as a general label which encompasses anyone who writes about food, restaurants, and cooking. "Food critic" is a more specific term for those who review restaurants from an evaluative stance and they often rely on a rating system to assess the meal. Criticism has an important value in marketing, tourism, and cultural experiences. A critic can often be thought a bit arrogant, and not as learned about the subject as a food writer might be. I think someone becomes a food critic because they're compelled to share their incredible enthusiasm for good food. Plus a need to remind the public that there is no reason not to dine well!

Venerated food writers like MFK Fisher and Julia Child truly know food; they talk about cooking, about meaning, about cultural revelance, the olfactory pleasure of making your mother's recipe. A writer will wax on about the memory of what was eaten on a first date, at least if the date goes well. That doesn't make a critic.

MFK Fisher wrote about food and life with no separation between the two. Julia Child, James Beard, Laurie Colwin, David Lebovitz, Patricia Wells, AJ Liebling, Elizabeth David, Calvin Trillin, Melissa Clark, Craig Claiborne, Michael Ruhlman and yes Anthony Bourdain (and the list goes on) have all influenced many a cook and literary food practitioner with their insightful comments on the history of modern food, how to cook as well as how we consider food in our lives.

Restaurant critics use analytical thinking, but they don't necessarily go on about the philosophy behind food and the emotional content. To be a good restaurant reviewer, you need to write about what the food meant to you, evaluate the meal, and communicate that experience to other people.

Bryan Miller, the food critic for the New York Times from 1985 to 1993, wrote reviews that were exciting to read, like mini-novellas. He wrote with generosity and intelligence; the writing was clever, succinct, and he was definitely enlightened about food. An example: "The qualities of an exceptional cook are akin to those of a successful tightrope walker: an abiding passion for the task, courage to go out on a limb and an impeccable sense of balance." You understand exactly what he means and almost hold your breath a little in appreciation. Both food writers and critics need to engage their reader in that way.

The Food Writing Industry

Food culture moves in various ways – one movement is happening, and then suddenly another trend takes over. There's a huge alliance of people who write food blogs, use Twitter, and write content for online articles. Food Blogger conferences are popping up all over the country and there are tutorials, talks, a community of shared experiences and problem solving. There is an industry, but there's not necessarily a guarantee to make a lot of money. That's more for celebrity chefs! Food has become more than the accessory du jour, it has invaded the small screen, the news, it's the festival focus for weekend fun…

As I began exploring more opportunities for food writing I happened to meet Ryan D'Agostino, the food editor for Esquire magazine and an author in his own right. We started talking about restaurants and cooking at a dinner party and we became friends. From time to time, I would ask him for advice. I learned that the industry is really slotted into categories. What Esquire magazine focuses on will be different than what Vogue focuses on which is going to be different than what a food chat/blog focuses on.

I've always been obsessed by food. When Chowhound first started back in the nineties I was in on that from the beginning. I lived for it, I loved to respond to everyone's postings, I couldn't wait to continue a conversation, and see what others were talking about. While I was working at another career, I'd be online and would sneak over to some food website, checking to see what they were up to and getting involved. I'd always enjoyed writing and had taken creative and critical classes in college, so the territory wasn't unfamiliar.

Now there are a plethora of food communities online. There's a great forum called mouthfulsfood.com. People have long, intense discussions about a slice of pizza and what it means, it goes on and on. Some people think that it's nuts, but I think it's completely energizing and fascinating. You're either in or you're not. Then there are sites like Yelp – it seems to be a lot of people sitting in the dark saying mean or uninformed things. You don't know what their taste is, how balanced their evaluation is, or whether their opinion is accurate or meaningful. You need to be careful about who you follow. Read enough of anyone's opinions to see if you can rely on them.

You don't do this for money, you don't become an actor because you think you'll be famous, you do it because you love acting, and you want to be those characters and say those words. Food writing generates an enthusiastic ardor and as food is so much about culture, security, and love, writing about it is a manifestation of that.

Food
Writing
Skills

Steps To Becoming A Successful Food Writer

There's more than one path to a career as a food writer, but the most important thing is to distinguish yourself from the pack. Find out what is competitive, but then discover what makes you distinct from that. What are you passionate about? What food do you love? What happening do you want to capture? If you stick to what you love, your excitement and strength will shine through your writing.

Take it all in: the flavors that your experience aromatically, on your tongue, the combination of ingredients, the colors on the plate. Learn more about the food you love and how it is made. Revel in curiosity, taste and discovery. Write from a position of experience. Seek out the new and unique, but don't get into competition over who is the most unconventional.

Read books by great food writers, read legendary cookbooks, and have food reference books at your side. Think about what *you* are bringing to the table. Food is communication. It speaks to your heart and to your past. It helps you forge new relationships and relish old ones.

The seminal book on Mediterranean food, *Honey from a Weed*, written by Patience Gray, isn't just recipes: it's about how to live. Her writing reveals our curiosity for life, our fears, and our desires. Plus the perfect pistou recipe!

As with many occupations in this world, knowing about a variety of subjects makes a big difference in your interpretation of a meal, and how you present that perception. Having a sense of humor, a background in literature, art, music, history and current politics are all part of what makes for a good story about anything as well as food. Critics and writers are now playing a responsible role in today's sustainable food culture. With chefs and restauranteurs now leading a successful soft revolution to support healthy eating and sustainable farming, critics are taking on the issue by educating the general public about what they are actually eating. Know what's happening in the world and how it relates to you and food.

Dine out, cook, and explore food trends. Look at artisan foods that are now taking a star position at markets and festivals. Visit farmer's markets and speak with the farmers – see what's happening out there.

But the most important step: write. Just write. About anything really and eventually move on to the subject of food. Get comfortable with your words and how you want to share your observations.

Essential Qualities of Food Writers

A great dinner isn't just about the food: it's almost a subliminal experience qualified by keen interest, good conversation at the table, and satisfaction with the meal. You need to capture that encounter and communicate it to the reader through fresh language and balanced observation. Food writers use their knowledge of food to inform the consumer. The writing needs to come from an experienced background: people who know how to cook or at least understand the process and who know what the ingredients are. If you understand how different herbs and spices interplay, you can more easily articulate the nuance of a recipe or a dish.

If you're going to write about something, and expect a readership, you need to stay current on the topic. Seek out and explore the current trends. Follow the news, note what's being offered by food artisans and farmers and see if you can spot the next wave. There are festivals in New York every weekend, and you can go crazy with all the homemade dishes. There's so much going on right now with inventive fare. There's a guy in Brooklyn who makes bacon marmalade; he was the first person I know doing that. Now everything you can think of is made with bacon. That fad will eventually pass, so to stay on the cutting edge, you might assume the role of food detective and try to recognize the next happening cuisine or ingredient.

Liking or disliking a meal isn't enough. You have to be expansive in your thinking: don't limit your palate. Describe a meal in ways other than yummy, a word I've grown to detest. If you're going to talk about food you need to understand what it means, how it got to the plate, and what the motive of the chef was. Take it all in.

It's important to understand that dining at a clam shack on some pier, enjoying a freshly caught fish simply sauced with parsley, good olive oil and lemon can be perfection – because it is a dish at the peak of its taste. And to also know that a chef like Wylie Dufresne of WD-50 in New York City creates a plate with seven different components meant to be tasted as one bite – taking your mouth on a divine adventure from sour to sweet to salty to sweet to bitter to spicy to salty again. Each dish makes you feel deliriously alive and grateful to be having it but one took hours to create and one ten minutes. Note the quality, the ingredients, and the intention.

Elements of Good Writing

With food writing, you don't want to be vague. Consider the various textures and tastes, and make comparisons to tell your story. Words like "delicious," "awesome" and "amazing" are not descriptive. Salty and spicy are fine to use but why not try piquant, brackish, refreshing, zesty, tangy, and so on.

Think about a piece of music you like, the mood it puts you in, and the way it makes you feel – those same words can apply to food. Choose an item like a fruit or dessert or whatever appeals to you and make a list of words that you free associate with to describe it, then add those words to your adjective list. You'll be surprised by the word choices that you will find as well as how they apply across the board.

Heighten the tastebuds of your readers. Consider these two sentences: "It was the yummiest spaghetti with clams, it was amazing and delicious and kind of creamy." But perhaps the next sentence would have a reader dialing for a reservation…"Handmade linguine bathed in white wine, beautifully roasted whole garlic cloves and the briny essence of clams is dense and chewy, while crushed red peppers play footsie with the back of your tongue."

With writing exercises, don't second guess yourself – just write. It doesn't have to be perfect or even good, but it has to come from your voice. Skip the beginning if you can't get started; go into the body of what you need to communicate. Be open to new ideas, and move on when you get stuck.

If you want to write about a particular meal but you can't seem to begin, jump in and start writing about the piece of steak, the way the potatoes were cooked, what it was like to sit at that table. Was it comfortable, loud, warm or cold? Start by picking out things you feel familiar with. Eventually you'll start writing with ease about your actual experience.

Finding Your Voice

Have courage in your convictions. I've always been very opinionated, but I feel that I'm opinionated and fair. I don't need to trump your opinion, I'm just clear about mine. Know what you like and why and then be able to back it up. Nobody knows everything, and people have their specialties, but it's important to have the courage to state an informed opinion.

Spike Lee once said of his early days in filmmaking, that when he was first in a room with studio executives, he got the feeling "that they all thought making a movie was a mystical process known only to three white men and he thought – don't you just need a camera and an attitude?" Just like food writing.

Stay open and present to your experiences. Be clear about what you think, but be open to what other people say, because your mind can be changed. No one can make you like a food you hate, but if you try it cooked in different ways, you might find something about it you enjoy.

A Day
In
The
Life
Of A
Food
Writer

What's It Really Like To Be A Food Writer

Lifestyle

Eat. Food trucks are on every corner, pop-up dining venues are constantly appearing helmed by the infamous wanting to branch out and the less known who want to be recognized. There are themed dining clubs, secret kitchen gatherings, fields with long tables and happy people, rooftop dessert cliques all there for you to partake in and learn from.

In today's food climate, there are events galore to attend, symposiums on growing your own dinner, vendor meet-ups, groups like the Gastronauts, a club for adventurous eaters (www.gastronauts.net) and podcasts that disseminate every last sensory blitz of any and all foods like The Sporkful (www.thesporkful.com). Immerse yourself in the world of food and dining and find what interests you. Check out a site like www.foodevents.com which lists goings on all around NYC but often includes exotic culinary traditions happening elsewhere.

Have your notepad at the ready. It's hard to retain every last detail from decor to service to each dish, you have to develop a shorthand for yourself so you can easily keep track of the meal at the table. Sometimes a checklist is helpful, your personal Cliff Notes that enable you to easily write your review later.

Explore, observe, pop off the sofa, get lucky. One of my favorite finds was Little Pepper, a Chinese restaurant in Flushing, Queens – I found it when I was looking for a restaurant that had previously been at that address and I showed up the day they opened. Someone with me spoke Chinese, which was fortunate because there was no English written or spoken. A group of us went once a week for a long time because the food was that addicting. Eventually they added a menu in English.

Day to Day Activities

Most critics and bloggers eat out at least 7 or 8 times a week. Your day might start off with checking in with your favorite blogs and websites. Part of your quest is to recognize other food writers by confirming or rejecting what they are saying. You want to insert yourself into the mix and make sure that you're not in a culinary vacuum. Then you have to consider what you're going to write about: an old favorite that has fallen off the world's radar, that new awning just uncovered on a side street yesterday, or what your editor assigns you.

If the review is for my personal blog or website, I don't go to a restaurant four times before writing about it. However, if I was going to review it for something bigger in scope like Esquire or the New York Times, I'd base my report on numerous occasions. You don't want to judge based on one experience, particularly if it's a bad one. You have to be careful, but it's often not possible to afford several visits. Let's put it this way: I don't review Le Bernardin, unless someone's taking me there! But I will go to Elmhurst, Queens and eat at a Malaysian place where dinner costs $20, and repeat visits are not an extravagance.

One tip is to get on a list with restaurant publicists, and they will invite you to soft openings. A soft opening is during the early days of a restaurant before the general public is invited. You get to acquaint yourself with a restaurant without paying for it, and with no obligation to write about it. It's also a great way to open a dialogue with other food writers and meet people in the industry.

Salary Potential

Your salary potential varies considerably based on the outlet – whether you're writing for a glossy magazine, a local newspaper, a national venue, a website, or whatever media. It also will depend on your expertise and your resume.

You can expect six figures at a major outlet, a hundred bucks for a review in a local paper, two bucks a word at many magazines, and anywhere from a few dollars to a few thousand in ads for bloggers. Don't go into food writing for the money – do it because you love it.

A Guide To Restaurant Reviews For Food Critics

Restaurant Reviews 101

The oft forgotten idea about a food critic is that they exist to sell newspapers, not sell restaurants. So though their star may be aligned with a chef, or a fabulous meal – their purpose is to keep people paying for the paper that a critic's opinion is plastered on.

I start thinking of ideas on the way home, and sometimes I take notes on my phone. Usually as I'm eating some catchphrase from a movie or song sticks in my head and I start to build my review around that. It becomes my hook. I always know what I want to comment on, what stood out for me. You have to divine what's important to you. Everyone has things that they look for and value. For me it's the overall experience, and of course whether or not I like the food. I don't think you need a criteria list, I prefer a more holistic approach.

For the initial review, I write very quickly. Then I spend time rewriting. For the first draft I'll use anything and everything – side comments, metaphors, even jokes. It's like a grocery list – you write everything down and then you decide what you feel like carrying home. Revision takes longer than initial writing. I get all my ideas out of my head, and then shaping it takes time and thought.

Keep a little list of every place you go. If you don't have the time to review every single restaurant, write brief sentences. Reduce the critique to its essence.

I once kept a journal that was only one line a day. If there was something really incredible, I would write three sentences. I don't always remember every detail, but I do know what I liked, didn't like and what the general tone of the experience was. You can always look up the menu later if you forget exact components of a dish.

Finding the Best Restaurants to Review

There are enough blogs and tweets to follow where you can learn about new places but it's important to develop your own instincts and discover some yourself. I read a lot so that I can know what people are talking about and what is up and coming. Get in before the buzz.

I follow all kinds of food people on Twitter and if they really like a place, of course I want to try it. If it's new and I appreciate the pedigree of the chef or the history of the restaurateur, then I want to go there. I always have a list of places I can't wait to investigate and the order changes all the time. From first position to tenth position and back again depending on what else suddenly comes down the pike.

Get to places before the rush. It's like seeing a Broadway show before opening night. While the jury is still out, everyone is doing their best work. No one has been deflated or too pumped up by the reviews. You get to have a true experience.

Reviews can change a restaurants perception and sometimes actually influence the cooking. Kitchens always need to evolve but sometimes it's not in the right direction. I like to form my own opinions before I hear too many details.

Keep a balance in your restaurant list between different types of cuisine. Explore new ethnic restaurants – they're often much less expensive. I keep a separate list for when I'm willing to spend more money.

Food writers should mix it up. I love a good dive, and I'm happy to be sitting on a stool on a dirt floor. But I'm also happy to be somewhere that's the top of the line in terms of quality and service.

Identifying & Working With Your Culinary Biases

Food writers, like anyone else are not going to love every kind of food. Usually you have to grin and bear it and just make it work – so to speak. It's important to remember that chefs draw inspiration from a variety of sources and it's that plus technique and staying open to innovative cuisines that keep us diners satisfied, appreciative and entertained. So we can bridge the bias gap too.

On the flip side, Top Chef Masters winner, Chef Floyd Cardoz was recently interviewed on the blog The Sweet Beet (www.thesweetbeet.com) and when asked "How do you cook differently when you're feeding diners verses feeding yourself? " had this to say: " I don't. When I cook, I want to be happy with what's on the plate. For example, I hate cream so I don't use cream for my guests and I don't use cream for myself."

Personally, I'm not big into offal and organs but certainly appreciate and applaud those who can't wait to dig into brain. I support all manner of eating and really do respect the idea of cooking every edible part of an animal. I have great resources among friends and colleagues – fellow diners who will forge right through animal gut and whom I trust implicitly so I can rely on their opinions for my clients.

I'm an equal opportunity food enthusiast. And I'm excited when anyone is properly sated regardless of whether or not it's something I enjoy. It's all part of the major bonding that sharing food seems to inspire.

Restaurant Review Rating Systems

The Holistic Food Critic

Using a Food Rating System

Everyone needs a reference point if they're trying to get started. Templates are helpful because they reduce fears. You realize that you only have to answer a certain set of questions. It's important to create your own checklist. Include the obvious ones:

Vitals:
Address, phone, neighborhood, hours of operation, credit cards, general cost level, reservations, occasion or style (casual, formal, fun night out, etc), pricing, outdoor space or not.

Decor:
Atmosphere, ambience, colors, lighting, style, seating (comfortable or not), music, sound level. Is it hip, sedate, casual, formal? What's the crowd like? Who dines here?

Service:
Was your reservation honored? Were you shown to your table on time? Was your server helpful? Knowledgeable? Do you know your server's first name? Do you want to? Did your server hover, refill water glasses too often or not enough? Did they fill wine glass properly?

Food:
What's the concept/intention for the food, and was it carried out? What kind of ingredients? Unusual, complex, organic? Portion size? Price commensurate with level of food? Name a few favorite dishes (or what you disliked) and describe for appearance, flavor balance, creativity. What are some popular dishes at the restaurant?

General Tone:
Offer positive and negative thoughts. Tell anything noteworthy about the experience as a whole from your perspective.

Make sure you address these basics, but include something personal for you. What was important to you? What did you respond to? Readers will come to you for your unique perspective, not just the generic framework of a review.

If you're writing for a magazine, newspaper, or blog with an established rating system, you need to adjust to their scale. Most use a star system – no stars can mean ordinary to bad, one star is good, two stars is very good, three stars is excellent, and four is off the charts.

Editors want to know if the food is good of course, but they are equally concerned with the restaurant's atmosphere, reservation policy, and available parking – specific concerns that readers have.

Top Tips for Restaurant Reviews

Try to suss out what intention a chef or restaurant might have and whether or not they have accomplished their goal. Do some research on the restaurant – who is the owner? Where has the chef worked before? How does this place differ from earlier restaurants? What is its niche? What are the signature dishes?

Tell a story with your review. Robert McG. Thomas was a New York Times journalist who happened to find the unlikely specialty of being a wonderful obituary writer. He focused on the more obscure deaths of the 1990's and he did so with incredible wit and irony. His observations were intimate and respectful. I always found myself looking forward to the latest entry and would become completely absorbed by the esoteric life he would reveal with nuanced humor and appreciation.

You might wonder why I would equate the summation of a life to a write-up meant to entice patronage of a dining establishment but I'm not so far off – grab hold of your reader, make them wonder where you might be leading them, envelop them in your fervor. Mr. Thomas made you empathize with the life he revealed. If you can invite your reader to follow along, feel like a guest at your table, and be excited to see what's next – they will trust you and listen to what you have to say.

Food Critic Anonymity

There are only about three people in the world that might need to be anonymous! Obviously a New York Times critic could be treated more extravagantly than the average customer, but it's not as if food bloggers and magazine writers in general will be the recipient of that kind of largesse.

On the other hand, once when I had emailed a pop-up restaurant from my eatquestnyc address, my table was offered many extra tidbits and tastes. I assumed that the hosts were just really nice people, but a friend said, "They may be treating you better because they think you're going to write about them."

Food
Reviews

How To Evaluate The Food

You need to consider presentation, consistency, and flavor balance. Is the food under or overcooked? Intense spicy heat in a dish doesn't work if it's just too hot. The heat should bring out the essence of the food. The beauty about salt is that it brings flavors forward, but it is easy for chefs to go overboard. An acid, like lemon or lime will brighten a fish or vegetable. Calibrating flavor has everything to do with an integration of spices and herbs that bring out the true nature of a dish, its terroir. Like with wine, it's the special characteristics of a combined taste that define a dish and make it unique.

When you order your meal, it's best to try a little bit of everything. Friends joke that I can feed a small nation by what I order. I usually go with four or five people, and try out as many dishes as we can. If you need to know the consistency of the place, go back several times, because you don't want it to be a fluke that once it was fantastic. Not every food blogger is going to go to a place four or five times – but sometimes if you really like it, you bring back different friends.

I want to feel the chef's sense of pride as those plates come out of the kitchen.

The Price Factor

Cost matters – readers want to know the value of their meals. People have less time and less money than they used to – they don't want to blow it on a choice in the Zagat guide that might be outdated or unreliable. In your review, show the range of prices for the appetizers, the entrées, and the desserts. You can also use a cost rating system to show value – $ for cheap places, $$ for inexpensive, $$$ for moderately priced spots, and $$$$ for expense accounts.

Food doesn't cost as much to make as the price listed – what people are paying for is the overall experience, the comfort of being taken care of. If the restaurant is expensive, the food needs to be spectacular. I often arrive at places with a list of dishes that people are talking about. I like to know what the signature dish is and what can't be missed.

Restaurant Comparisons

When I'm at a new restaurant, I try to stay present with the experience, but one can't help but compare similar places. There are five billion pizza places which say they do Neapolitan pizza, and it's just not true. So when you go to one, rank it against others that profess the same.

Ask yourself which one you like better? Why? Compare the restaurants on several levels – if one costs more, is it worth it? Is the crust authentic by Neapolitan standards? Which décor is better? Which appealed to your overall satisfaction ?

However, you can't compare restaurants with very different objectives. With pizza, you may prefer a thin crust, so you can't compare it to a deep dish pizza joint. Be clear to your readers about your preferences, so they can determine what to take away from your review. Try to group your comparisons together, whether it's by neighborhood, style of cuisine, or price range.

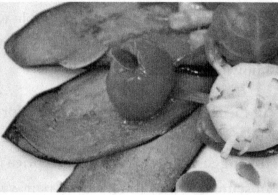

Wine Reviews

How To Evaluate The Wine

Wine Lists

I look for value-driven lists with wines I know from importers that I like. If the restaurants you review are known for their wine list, familiarize yourself at home with the different styles of wine. That's a much more affordable way to try out various wineries. Which wine you drink will depend on your meal, but it's best if you go into the wine list with comfortable knowledge.

At the restaurant, make sure to ask for the right wine person to discuss your options. Ideally this is the wine buyer or the sommelier on duty. Do you like it lighter or fuller-bodied? Ask for suggestions that match your price range. See if there is anything out of the ordinary or obscure that they think would pair well with the particular choices of the guests.

If the sommelier suggests the most expensive wine on the list, you know you are talking to the wrong wine person. Ask for another suggestion if you don't feel comfortable asking for someone else to recommend.

Trick up the sleeve: bring a friend who actually knows good wine. You can use that expert to judge whether you're being given good direction. People at restaurants are open to amateurs and people who are less knowledgeable, so don't be afraid. But don't write about something you don't know about.

Advice for Non-Drinkers

These days so many people don't drink. Dishes are created for the mouth feel and taste of a diner based on the components and chemistry of the food. Not because of the right wine. Though wine, like salt, can make certain dishes pop in your mouth, neither wine nor any alcohol is necessary to get the full dining experience.

Often now the health conscious get to experiment with elixirs, combinations of more exotic juices, simple syrups and sodas. Find the right variation to accompany your meal and write about that. Make a non drinker feel included by what they can have not by what they can't.

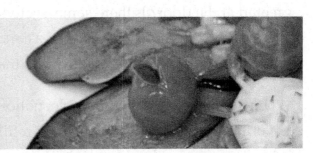

Restaurant Service Reviews

How To Evaluate The Service

When I write about a restaurant's service, I try to get a holistic sense of the place. I want to feel well taken care of without seeing anyone around me. It starts at the beginning – how did they take your reservations? Were they polite, patient, clear? When you arrive, how are you greeted at the door? Is there somewhere to comfortably wait if your table isn't ready or they don't take reservations? An offer of a conciliatory drink goes a long way to erase a delay in being seated. Be attentive and express the whole experience to your reader.

When you are seated at your table, notice how the wait staff is trained. I don't want anybody hovering, and I don't want my water refilled with every sip nor my wine glass filled to the brim. The servers shouldn't be in your face, but if you have to find a waiter you want to know that you can.

Asking a waiter to make recommendations can be risky. If the waiter doesn't eat fish, and you do, their advice isn't going to be helpful – they can't account for your taste, whether you like it spicy or bland, overdone, raw. It can be a helpful way to determine the restaurant's signature dishes, but sometimes waiters push food for other reasons, the kitchen may have ordered too much of one thing.

Once at a well-known restaurant in Manhattan, I asked the sous-chef what he would recommend, and he went into a long description about how the salmon was hand-delivered weekly by members of a tribe of Indians, and I thought, *How does that affect the food?* That didn't persuade me to order the salmon. You don't want pretentiousness in the presentation. It depends on the length of the review, but I generally only focus on the service if it's incredibly great or incredibly bad.

A fantastic meal becomes disappointing if the service falls below the standard of the food. Besides good manners, a server who can connect to the diner will succeed in making them satisfied and happy.

Restaurant Ambience Reviews

How To Evaluate The Ambiance

When you evaluate a restaurant's ambiance, consider your first impressions. What message is the restaurant trying to convey? Is it a dive? A homey, country-style kitchen? An upscale, chic restaurant? When you are finished with your meal, you can decide whether the restaurant has succeeded in its intentions. There's a German word *gemütlich* which translates as cozy, comfortable, pleasant. I want to feel that – a sense of contentment, a true emotional fit.

Presentation is everything. From the moment you pass through the door until you're seated at your table. There's the welcome you're offered by the staff, the decor and what that mood conveys, and then even before you get to the food – there's the question of the menu. Whether it's chalkboard or woven raffia, the menu should reflect the focus and the ambience of the restaurant by the design, the description of the food and of course the pricing. Are you seated at a "good" table verses one behind a column by the swinging kitchen door?

I love a good dive, extra bright lighting and all, but in general, lighting can make all the difference in your design comfort. The longtime complaint of needing a lit match to read your menu is valid, and so is looking good as you sit across from your companions. I have close friends who wouldn't go to a place with fluorescent lighting – for some people it really affects the way the food tastes. Ideally a restaurant strikes a balance with soft lighting that is soothing but bright enough to see what you are eating.

Comfortable seating matters more to some people than others. There's a Korean barbecue place I love with fantastic food but tiny uncomfortable stools. It's important to let your readers know this ahead of time. Many people have bad backs, and the quality of the food will go unnoticed if they are uncomfortable throughout the meal.

Consider the noise levels of the restaurant. Louder restaurants have more energy, but if you are recommending a place for a date, readers will want to be able to carry on a conversation. Make a note in your review if there is a background soundtrack, and whether it is distracting or not or is it indistinct chatter and clinking cutlery that surrounds you? Ideally you'll be able to hear the little murmurs of joy as your table dines.

Dining out comes with the edict of a langorous mood, time to enjoy the table. Rushed service is a definite turn off, no one wants to be cattle prodded out the door. Everyone has a discomfort threshold and you can personalize your review by including your own. I loathe dining across from a mirror – I really don't want to watch myself eat.

Does it feel like someone has created a home that you've been invited into? Is the restaurant seeking customers or repeat clients? Is there a personality that has been consciously conceived? All of these elements indicate a level of care and that care translates to my perception of the experience.

Writing Food Articles & Building Your Portfolio

Thriving As A Food Writer

Build Your Portfolio

If food writing is what you love, pursue it – but know that you aren't guaranteed a full time career. Keep your day job, and work on your writing portfolio at night. Reach out to local newspapers, magazines, and websites, and offer to cover food festivals in your area. Going local can be hard in New York City, but there are handouts and free dailies. Papers like the Village Voice while free, might not be open to freelancers. Also look up local websites like Citysearch, or the Citysearch version for your town. It helps to have a specific focus that fills a genre gap and original content is key.

Show your work to the food editor, and see if they take it. If it's good enough and *short* enough, they might print your work. Remember that most food pieces are brief, and editors won't have room for a long essay. Keep it concise.

When you approach a food editor, offer yourself on a trial basis. Ask the editor: let me write four pieces for you, and see if you like them. If the newspaper, magazine, or blog gets a good response to your work, they may contract you for additional content.

Offer to write press releases for new restaurants. Reach out to the owners, and show them a sample of your work. Remember that your goal is to draw customers, so keep your language lively and succinct.

Airline magazines are another great resource – they are always looking for more content. Write about upcoming festivals and new culinary trends. Time your article to the season – make sure you offer the right content at the right time. You don't want to be writing about good picnic spots for a magazine that will be printed in the winter.

Be Persistent With Your Work

Research the magazines and websites that you like, and ask the editors for their guidelines. Use those instructions to direct your work, and create a portfolio of different lengths – 50 words, 100 words, 500 words, 1000 words. If you want to write for a certain magazine, newspaper, or website, read their past issues. Get to know the audience, and which articles have gotten a lot of buzz.

Freelance is tough because you're giving away some content for free, but you have to give it up to get somewhere. Food critics are not hired to help restaurants; they're hired to sell newspapers. Think about what you're doing, and who you're writing for. They want subscriptions, and sales – attracting people is the quest. You want to bring all that to the ready.

Be persistent – it's imperative. You can't listen to "no" and be discouraged. Try again with a new idea, or a different presentation. Try focusing on a specific subject, for example an article directed toward single men. Think about what's appealing to them, perhaps create an at home dinner menu for a date. Know your market.

What can you offer as far as unusual trends? What have you noticed with street food, at restaurants, or in grocery stores? Be willing to contribute anything and everywhere. You might not make a lot of money from freelancing, but as you gain experience, you will start trusting yourself.

A query letter has a basic premise to always be followed:

1. Let the editor know who you are by way of a one or two sentence introduction, ie: I am a student in culinary school, I am a chef at the Four Seasons in NYC, I'm a sanitation engineer with a dream.

2. What's your pitch? Why are you writing? Let them know in one sentence why you want them to consider you: I will write a day in the life of a culinary student. I will write about what celebrities order. I will write about the new secret lounge behind the recycling plant.

3. A short explanation of your experience with a mention of an article or two.

4. Don't ramble on, no one wants to read every idea you ever had or everything you've ever done. Make it brief.

5. Offer your article on spec or include two short pieces as an example of your writing style. If this is a cooking based query, include at least four recipes that you have actually created.

- Always send your query to the correct person at the magazine, newspaper or website.
- Make sure that above all else – you spell their name correctly. In fact be sure that your entire proposal is spelled correctly, anyone reading it will want to be clear that you're professional and that you take the time to appear so (even if you're not!).
- If you don't hear back from the editor, wait ten days before contacting them. If you don't

connect, you may try one more time to establish contact. If that fails, don't give up, just give up harassing this particular person.

Take Advantage of Social Media

Get into a dialogue with people on social media. Use all forms of it – blogs, Twitter, Foursquare, Tumblr, Youtube, Facebook, and any upcoming forms of media. Be consistent – put yourself out there on a regular basis. You don't want your readers to get bored and find another person to follow. Be careful, social media has also made everyone a critic. Opportunity abounds but earn your reader's trust.

Someone once said to me that Facebook is like a family reunion, and Twitter is like a cocktail party. On Twitter you can say: I love this restaurant, I like what you said, or I disagree, and get into a dialogue with them. It's like walking up to a stranger, and I think that that's an exciting prospect.

The more that you communicate with people, charge your thinking process, and write about your observations, the more you'll have something to say that others might want to follow. It's through these exchanges that you essentially make yourself appear.

Food Blogs

Tips For Successful Food Blogging

Building An Audience

Everyone has a secret. Sometimes the "hush hush I won't even tell myself" desire is something you wish you were. Like the lead singer in an outrageous rock band, or the ballerina on pointe who's barely earthbound. I actually loved what I did before succumbing to my obsession with all things food. While I'd be researching something for a design client, I'd suddenly find myself hours behind having been perusing online food boards and joining in a fast paced chat about Thai cuisine in Woodside. Time would slip by.

For years I'd been the go to person for friends, acquaintances and strangers I'd meet walking my dog – pretty much anyone trying to figure out where to dine, what to do for a special evening, how to find the perfect ingredient for that esoteric dish, THE burger, THE slice, THE gelato or Dutch licorice.

Working in the theatre many moons ago, none of us had any money. There was no information superhighway, so we would wander the streets for entertainment and randomly come upon a little jewel of a restaurant. The "soon-to-be-hip-and-trendy" before that was a catchphrase or a concept. We'd scrounge up the money to eat as many places as we could and then as I was always the most obsessed and intrigued – would tell everyone, you have to have to have to try this place.

I never minded people asking my advice. It was relaxing and absorbing to figure out where they should go and what they should have. Cut to the recession of several years ago when I officially decided to take a forever hiatus from one career and fall away into another.

Starting a Food Blog

Find a hook: a cooking with kids blog, a blog about Mexican hors d'oeuvres, a "what-to-make-when-you-and-your-new-partner-are-hungry-at-2am" blog. Do something that sets you apart. You're selling your take on food.

I started my own blog kicking and screaming, because I really didn't want one. There are so many blogs out there, but the only way to continue the conversation is to keep talking. Blogging means you have something to say, to share. The thing about a blog is that you have to have a focus. On my blog, I'm trying to sell a service, which are my recommendations. If you're bound and determined to dive in, you need to know what your angle is because you're selling your perspective. You can always expand, or start another one, but it's hard to command a following unless you have a clear viewpoint.

To attract people you have to rely on social media – Twitter, Facebook, and so on. The more that you connect online, and develop relationships, the more people will take notice of you. Look around at different blogging platforms and see which appeals to you most. I chose WordPress because I like its clean aesthetic.

How often should I post?

You have to write even when you don't want to. Just do it! A blog is an intelligent conversation, and you need to have someone to converse with. Ask a question – work breeds more work. You can't be quiet by yourself and wait for greatness to knock on your door. Be careful that you're not slanderous, and that you can back up what you say.

You don't have to write a long blog every day, but it's beneficial to at least do a short piece. Twitter a few times a day. Tweet about someplace you just ate, or pop into a discussion with someone about a lobster roll truck. If you don't keep it up, then people will drop back and get bored – you need to maintain an audience. Twitter is one third business, one third personal and one third inspiration.

All this being said, it's okay to take a day off if you have nothing to say, but if you're going to have a blog you should have something to say. Generally it's good to post on a Sunday night or a Monday – people want to see new stuff at the start of the workweek.

Writing About Food – Your Own Food Column

Start a newsletter, a food blog, an online magazine or e-zine, start commenting on other food sites and writing for them. Connect with those around you who also live to eat.

Check out magazine websites and ask about guidelines for accepting new writers. Food and Wine is less receptive to queries than Saveur. It helps if you have an unusual idea, or can offer up an interview with a food artisan doing something crazy or unique with food – tell food editors at newspapers or magazines that you have something incisive and special to offer.

Know your market. Know your audience. Check if a publication or site accepts new writers, food essays, or ideas on unusual trends.

Be willing to contribute anywhere and write about anything local to attract attention and experience. There are so many sites and magazines dedicated to lifestyle and nightlife, meet up groups for dining out, and sites targeted for tourists. Anything food related is possible – from restaurant reviews to the latest in cookware. Travel is a big deal: ferret out the local haunts of less traveled countries and do queries to travel sites.

Food magazines have something called FOB – front of book. They are usually smaller pieces that range in word count from 50 to 400 words. You would do these "on spec" of course – you will send them the work "on speculation." Most outlets will want to see examples of published work and this kind of short piece writing allows you to solicit a food editor while letting them see what you've got to offer.

Here's an example FOB piece of mine:

"*A spring Saturday in Madison Square Park* *usually means lines at Shake Shack and the return of playground noise. But last Saturday also meant the annual Sikh Day Parade and Festival. The idea is to honor gurus and martyrs, but being the friendly group that they are, it was a dining bonanza for the rest of us — table after table of free food. Lightly oiled naan stuffed with tomato-infused chickpeas and potato. Sweet mini lassis. More chickpeas, this time seasoned with tamarind and green chili pepper and served with saffron rice. Spicy vegetable curry drizzled with a vibrant yellow yogurt sauce, creamy tofu spinach scooped into your mouth with delicate chapati. Domino-sized karah prashad, a remarkable and simple bite made from sugar, butter, flour, and water. Did I mention it was all free?*

"Watching everyone eat (and honor gurus and martyrs) were the newly installed statues by Antony Gormley, a series of bronze, naked men stationed on the sidewalks and, more dramatically, on more than twenty rooftops overlooking the park. They nodded their naked approval as we diners squinted upward while reaching for another handful of moong dal, a crunchy lentil snack that I will now eat forever."

It's a way to start an exchange with the magazine. They can get to know you and perhaps become interested in your work. You will have to come up with the goods, do the research and make sure you are giving your best version of a piece and a topic.

Sometime in the 1980's the NYT published a review of a then new Vietnamese place called Nha Trang that had opened on Baxter Street in New York's Chinatown. The review appeared in the Wednesday edition and by that evening there was a line of people all the way around the block waiting to get in the door of this very casual, semi subterranean eatery. We took our place anticipating the barbecued shrimp paste with sugar cane and the grilled pork to come, how did we know what to get excited about? We had our NYT tucked under an arm at the ready for ordering … and so did 90% of the people around us! The power of the restaurant review … it spoke and we all listened. And we still do.

Additional Resources

Example Restaurant Review #1: Tides (A Seafood Restaurant)

This hidden gem pops up unexpectedly amid the concrete. Let's celebrate the arrival of this Tiny Great Undiscovered Seafood Place in all its 22-seat glory before the inevitable long lines and longer waits. Yes, it's an iteration of the seaside fish shack. But TGUSP does it to the max. Ultra fresh seafood, fried oysters and clams in a batter so delicate and sweet it's practically guilt free. Perfectly cooked daurade with grilled haricots verts. A corn pudding seems like no big deal, a little golden square in the middle of a white plate; but it melts in your mouth, and the taste that lingers is the velvety essence of deep sweet summer. Yes, Virginia – there is a lobster roll. Beautifully cooked, on the appropriate toasted hot dog bun and at the moment, served with cucumber and dill; the ingredients will change with the seasons. The wine list has about 3 or 4 bottles of each color. A gorgeous white Bandol was a big hit at our table. Monday nights have no corkage fee so bring your own favorite bottle.

A tiny place, with a small but balanced menu and smaller but tasteful wine list, what they've created is a fun and stylish backdrop for an alumnus of Mary's Fish Camp to cook in and cook wonderfully. The ceiling is a mosaic of undulating bamboo skewers, the tables spark to life with inset candles, even the restroom sink is witty. Add delightful, warm attentive service from the owners/staff and you have an itsy bitsy resort on some fantasy sea. In lieu of a house in the Seychelles, I'll take it.

Example Restaurant Review #2: Little Pepper Szechuan Restaurant

If I could call a restaurant home – this would be it. I would come in after a long day and curl up by dishes beautifully balanced with spicy heat and an almost haunting taste. I would set my clock by the always delectable lamb with cumin and cilantro (a signature dish) and at night my head would rest on luxurious tofu alive with tongue melting peppercorns and crushed peanuts.

Almost six years ago I wandered down a flight of steep stairs looking for Spicy and Tasty (which had moved around the corner) and found myself on opening day of a brightly lit, bare boned, non english speaking sanctuary of insanely fantastic food. For these last years I've become addicted to the owner Jacy Wu and her husband's hosting and cooking. I have ferried many friends to flushing and tho I have a couple of other favorites – Little Pepper will always be my touchstone.

As they grew in popularity, they went from a menu written only in Chinese (luckily I have a friend from Szechuan) to a bilingual menu where you had to point and drag your finger if you weren't fluent and hope for the best. Sometimes you got a dish you might never have tried (huzzah for the zesty, piquant whole green peppers in salt & sour sauce!) now they have moved to College Point. Fancier digs, bigger kitchen, slight increase in cost but the food is as sublime as ever. The flavors are layered, complex and distinct as well as beautifully and not overwhelmingly peppered. Maybe the food is even better because the Wu's energy is very relaxed. And the restaurant sparkles. The menu is now completely in English and it isn't even sticky anymore! I could always locate my favorites on the hard to read bilingual menu of yore and I kind of miss that point and see what happens aspect – this is all much more organized, but I'll adapt.

It's not that I want this place to be flooded with non asian faces, and not like they need the business – you now need a reservation for a weekend table, but I'm amazed how it still flies a bit under the radar. All fine with me! The owners have bought the College Point building and are no longer planning on re-opening the Roosevelt Av location so they are thankfully here for the duration. Phew. Safe. There is no chance of them dumbing down their dishes, the cooking is not by formula so sometimes there's more spice than less and vice-versa but no crazy pendulum here. This is food that you can count on, be satisfied by and yes – grateful for. And don't even consider starting a meal without the cucumber in mashed garlic. The Little Pepper gods will know …

Book / Web / Twitter Recommendations For Aspiring Food Writers

Reference Books:

Larousse Gastronomique

Food by Waverly Root

The Oxford Companion to Food

Seminal and Fun Cookbooks:

Honey From A Weed by Patience Gray

Essentials of Italian Cooking by Marcella Hazan

Chez Panisse Vegetables by Alice Waters,

Zuni Cafe by Judy Rogers

Deborah Madison's *Local Flavors*

World Vegetarian by Madhur Jaffrey

Heart of The Artichoke by David Tanis

Around My French Table by Dorie Greenspan

The New York Times Cookbook by Amanda Hesser

Bistro Cooking by Patricia Wells

Food Memoir / Info

On Food & Cooking, Keys to Good Cooking by Harold McGee

Spoon Fed / How Eight Cooks Saved My Life by Kim Severson (food memoir)

Blood, Bones & Butter by Gabrielle Hamilton

Blogs:

davidlebovitz.com

chezpim.com

cannelle-vanille.blogspot.com

smittenkitchen.com

orangette.blogspot.com

Twitter people:

@kittenwithawhip (kat kinsman/cnn)

@francis_lam (salon/gilt taste)

@amandafreitag (chef)

@jennyhighlife (jenny miller/grubstreet)

@foodista (compendium of food sources, trends, recipes)

@robertsietsema (village voice)

@skeeternyc (food curated – videos etc re artisan food makers)

Websites:

pinkpignyc.com

findeatdrink.com

doshermanos.co.uk

eater.com

dinevore.com

101cookbooks.com

food52.com

Like What You're Reading? Spread The Word!

We're a small startup, so we rely on happy readers to help us grow (hopefully, that means you!).

Here are some specific ways you can contribute:

1. Share your success with us! Tell us how the book has helped you
2. Visit our website: www.bestbookonfoodwriting.com and comment on your favorite article
3. Ask our experts a question! We'll answer the best ones directly on the site
4. Send us your feedback or ideas at feedback@hyperinkpress.com!

To make it worth your time (and to thank you for bugging your friends/family), email us after you've done any of the above and we'll give you a **special bonus** as thanks. Trust us, it's worth it!

Thanks!

CHECK OUT MORE TITLES FROM OUR BEST BOOK SERIES!

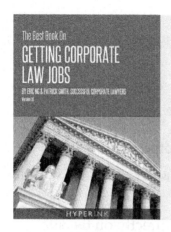

The Best Book On Getting Corporate Law Jobs

Want to learn the exact steps to getting a prestigious corporate law job? Interested in working for Davis Polk, Wilson Sonsini, and other top firms? Hear directly from the students that got in!

$25

BUY NOW

The Best Book On Getting Consulting Jobs In India

Want to learn the secrets of landing a consulting job at McKinsey, BCG, and Bain in India? A current Indian consultant shares his advice to navigating the recruiting process.

$25

BUY NOW

The Best Book On Naturopathy

Interested in becoming a naturopath? Julie Tran shares her stories and strategies for becoming a naturopathic doctor!

$25

BUY NOW

CPSIA information can be obtained at www.ICGtesting.com
Printed in the USA
LVOW03s0533120615

442162LV00009B/27/P